THE ULTIMATE TEACHER Appreciation GIFT BOOK

THE ULTIMATE TEACHER *Appreciation* GIFT BOOK

Create, Color, and Fill In a Year of Classroom Memories with the Best Teacher Ever

Illustrated by Annie Brock

Published in the United States by:
ULYSSES PRESS
P. O. Box 3440
Berkeley, CA 94703
www.ulyssespress.com

ISBN: 978-1-64604-026-1
Library of Congress Control Number: 2019951431

Printed in Canada by Marquis Book Printing
10 9 8 7 6 5 4 3 2 1

Managing editor: Claire Chun
Proofreader: Renee Rutledge
Cover design: Jake Flaherty
Cover illustrations: Annie Brock
Interior design and layout: Montague Monsters
Interior illustrations: shutterstock.com: © Gazoukoo; © Es sarawuth; © Bimbim; © balabolka; © edel; © josep perianes jorba; © rangsan paidaen; © Natalia Sheinkin; © peace_art; © Patty Chan

This book is for:

_____

From: _____

Grade: _____

Class of: _____

School: _____

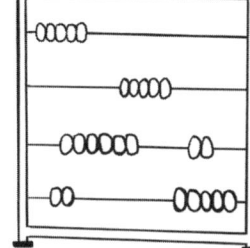

To me, you have been an amazing. . .

T ～～～～～～～～～～～～～～～～～

E ～～～～～～～～～～～～～～～～～

A ～～～～～～～～～～～～～～～～～

C ～～～～～～～～～～～～～～～～～

H ～～～～～～～～～～～～～～～～～

E ～～～～～～～～～～～～～～～～～

R ～～～～～～～～～～～～～～～～～

A picture so you'll always remember me:

  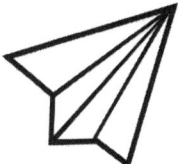

Five things I loved about my class were:

(Outline your hand and write one thing you loved in each finger.)

These are five things I
will remember about you!

But my favorite memory from this year is definitely:

_____

_____

_____

_____

_____

_____

To me, the avocation of a teacher has something elevating and exciting. While surrounded by the young, one may always be doing good.

Dorothea Dix

Coming to class every day made me feel:

_____

_____

_____

_____

_____

I really liked learning about:

_____

_____

_____

_____

_____

The funniest thing you said was:

_____

_____

_____

_____

_____

_____

But if I could go on any field trip
with you, it would be to:

_____

_____

_____

_____

_____

_____

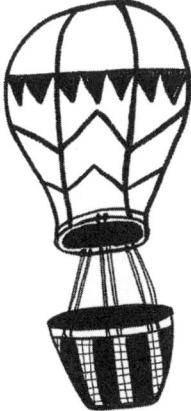

My favorite book we read in class was:

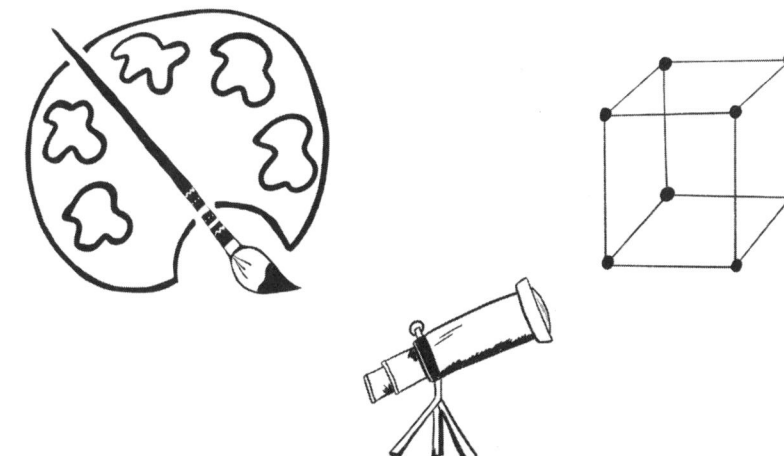

My favorite thing that we
learned about this year was:

_____

_____

_____

_____

Here is a picture from
one of my favorite days this year:

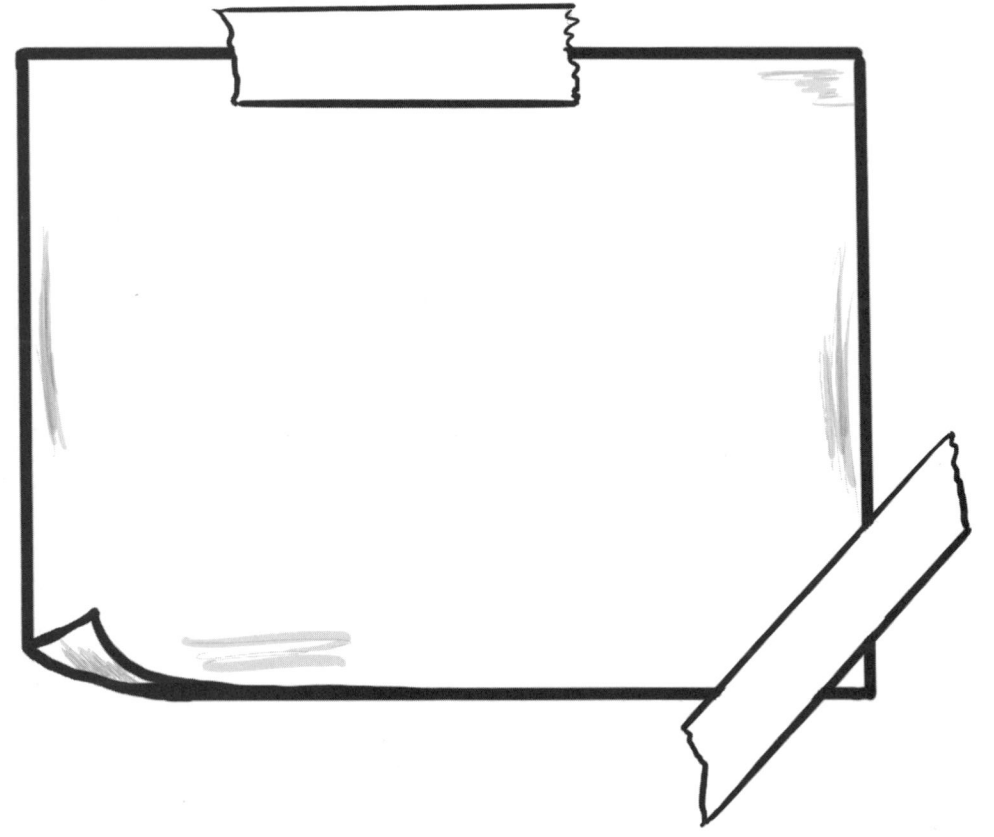

The best thing about being your student was:

_____

_____

_____

_____

The best thing about
having you as my teacher was:

_____

_____

_____

_____

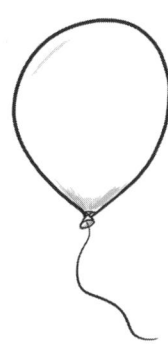

You are such a special teacher because:

_____

_____

_____

_____

 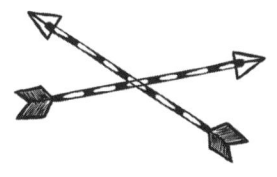

If you were a superhero, you would be:

_____

because. . .

_____

_____

_____

If you were an animal, you would be:

_____

because. . .

_____

_____

_____

If I could get you
anything in the world, it would be:

_____

_____

_____

_____

What I'm most excited about for next year is:

_____

_____

_____

_____

You deserve a special award

This

Teaching Award

is presented to

....

by ....

A Special Thank You

Dear _____,

Thank You!

_____

ABOUT THE ILLUSTRATOR

Annie Brock is a K–12 innovation specialist, and previously taught secondary English and creative writing. She is the coauthor of *The Growth Mindset Coach, The Growth Mindset Playbook, and In Other Words: Phrases for Growth Mindset.* Annie also wrote *Introduction to Google Classroom*. She lives in Holton, Kansas, with her husband, Jared, and their two children. Annie provided the illustrations for *The Growth Mindset Journal.*

DISCOVER MORE BEST-SELLING BOOKS FROM AUTHOR & ILLUSTRATOR ANNIE BROCK

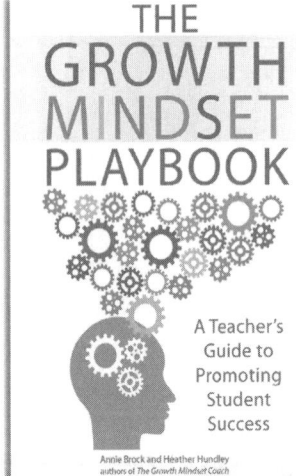
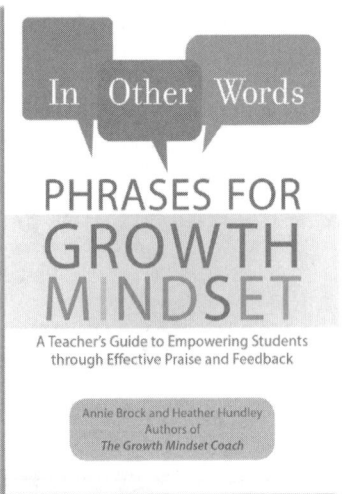

WWW.ULYSSESPRESS.COM